# Mental Health Guide for Busy Mums

Master the Art of Self Care and Transform Your Life

written and narrated by

ELA SENGHERA

Copyright © 2023 All rights reserved.

No content of this book may be reproduced or distributed without prior written permission from the author or the publisher.

Under no circumstances will any blame or legal responsibility be held against the publisher or author for any damages, reparation or monetary loss due to the information contained within this book, either directly or indirectly.

Legal notice

This book is copyright protected and is only for personal use. You cannot amend, distribute, sell, quote, use, paraphrase any part or the content within this book without the consent of the author.

Please note the information contained within this document is for educational and entertainment purposes only. All effort has been executed to present accurate, up-to-date, reliable and complete information. No warranties of any kind are declared or implied. Readers acknowledge that the author is not engaged in the rendering of legal, financial, medical, or professional advice.

By reading this book, the reader agrees that under no circumstances the author is responsible for any losses, direct or indirect, that are incurred. As a result of the use of information contained within this document, including but not limited to errors, omissions or inaccuracies.

## CONTENTS

*Introduction*   5

*Foreword*   7

1. Your Values System   9
2. The Power Of Your Mind   12
3. Challenge Your Beliefs   15
4. Your Relationships   19
5. Selecting Your Tribe   23
6. Does Your Mental Health Affect Your Children?   27
7. Managing Stress   32
8. Developing A Kind Inner Voice   36
9. Becoming Your Best Friend   38
10. Focus On Your Future   40

*Summary*   44

*Annex*   45

## *Dedication*

This book is dedicated to all mothers.

May you find joy and happiness in doing the most important job out there - raising children. I hope you build a beautiful, life-long relationship with your children, a relationship that is based on trust, love and mutual respect.

## INTRODUCTION

When two individuals, with different family backgrounds decide to live together under the same roof, there are bound to be some changes. Relationships, to be successful, require a series of adjustments by both partners. Things usually have a smooth start when a couple first gets together. People are generally good at handling their differences. However, things tend to change quickly when two people get married or decide to start a family together. New and unfamiliar circumstances can increase uncertainty and cause anxiety, which needs to be managed in the right way, for a relationship to survive.

Many people say that starting a family, as wonderful as it sounds, is a mixture of knowing yourself and learning to compromise. Raising children can make us feel fulfilled and happy but it can also be a process full of self-sacrifice and shifting priorities. This is the case for both parents, but especially for the mother.

Parenthood can be a source of joy as well as stress. The ability to adapt to this new role and new responsibility doesn't happen overnight. It requires time and patience. Although very few admit it, motherhood can be a tough journey through an unknown territory, where women learn to navigate through the peaks and troughs of life with little or no support and simply doing their best to avoid the big "pot holes" on the way. Sadly, many women lose themselves in the process of becoming a mother and a caretaker. Many of us are raised in a traditional way, believing that if we put the needs of other people above our own needs, our relationships will be a source of joy and happiness. Sadly, this rarely happens.

Many women feel out of control because they're constantly attending to the needs of others. While she is busy nurturing others, caring for them, a woman rarely gets nurtured herself. Far too often women lose their identity to the needs of others and eventually end up overworked, unfulfilled or emotionally drained. Those in happier relationships have a partner whose attitude and priorities match their own ones. Undoubtedly this makes the motherhood journey a little easier.

Our common belief that we women are born to be the primary caregiver to our children, partner and families, too often turns out to be nothing but a limiting belief, which works against us in the long term. Yet, this is so commonly observed in today's society. This traditional approach to women and men's responsibilities, can cause much dissatisfaction, self-neglect and a mountain of unfulfilled dreams and plans for many women. It can cause poor life satisfaction, depression or resentment, which when not dealt with, can contribute to poor health, relationship strain, and so often a divorce further down the line. In many cases unexpressed resentment can also cause various psychosomatic diseases or even cancer.

As a mother I know how overwhelming life can get. So often we struggle to stay on top of things, without neglecting our health or our relationships. In this book, I've put together my professional knowledge and personal experience, to help mums, like you, create more balance and fulfilment in their lives. This book is packed with exercises to help you navigate through your daily life challenges and put into practice your newly acquired knowledge, so that you can become a stronger, more resilient version of yourself.

## FOREWORD

*by Psych. MA Katie Price*

In my work as a Drama and Arts Therapist working in school settings I have met many children and young people who are experiencing challenges with their mental health. In many instances it quickly became evident that for my work to be effective, the family of the young person needs to be included in therapy.

There is, without a doubt, a connection between the mental health of a child and that of their surrounding family, typically including their mothers. Although a child's mental well-being is not solely dependent on their mother's wellbeing, maternal mental health is a large contributing factor to the state of every child's mental health. Sadly, this is not common knowledge.

There is an unrealistic expectation that the journey into motherhood will be that of a positive experience. Mothers will be able to adapt to this significant change without needing to address their mental well being. There is a strong belief that, as a mother, you will be able to provide, nurture, care-give and teach your children without addressing and nurturing your needs first, which needless to say does not serve many women well. These societal expectations are silent, rarely spoken about, but have a huge impact on the well being of every mother out there.

Yet, lack of self care in working mothers is one of the leading causes contributing to poor life satisfaction, increased levels of stress, anxiety, relationship strain, lower performance at work and depression. Many women are yet to learn the art of prioritising their own needs and acting on their desires. Let's remember that when a baby is born this new situation requires a lot of adjustment between partners and a real change of our priorities and our attitudes. And this change can cause lots of stress. Motherhood is a journey that has many learning curves. It requires a woman to be kind and gentle with herself, to show love and care to herself, to learn to set boundaries and trust her instincts. Self-care becomes an essential part of this process. By learning to prioritise her own needs, a woman takes an active part in the process of becoming her own friend, a happier mother and is therefore better positioned to be able to better care for others, including her children.

Childhood is a crucial time to create firm foundations which will influence the rest of a child's life. Self care allows a woman to have a positive impact on her children's emotional, cognitive, and behavioural development. Self care is something that needs to be prioritised and practised among women of all ages and all ethnic backgrounds.

I hope that the readers of this book will find connection through the author's lived experiences. As a busy mum herself, Ela speaks from experience in an honest and relatable tone. She addresses key areas of an individual's wellbeing, which not only supports us in our roles as mothers but also in every other aspect of our lives.

"Mental Health Guide for Busy Mums" is a very helpful resource which would benefit all mothers, everywhere, regardless of their backgrounds, past experiences or relationship with their mental health.

Well done for reaching out for this book! I hope it will inspire you to take the first steps towards yours and your family's well being and help you learn how to build happier and more fulfilling relationships.

# 1

# Your Values System

As you know we are all very different. What is important for you might not be important for me. We have different value systems and different priorities. Just because we are all women doesn't mean that we prioritise our families or our jobs in the same way. The need to be a mom first and working professional second isn't the same for all of us. This is why it's crucial that you take time to get to know yourself and understand your priorities and your highest values.

Human values underline every aspect of human behaviour. You could say that the hierarchy of our values dictate our destiny. Somebody said *"Tell me what your values are and I'll tell you where you are going."* If you really want to know how to empower your life and do something extraordinary with it - find out what your highest values are first. Finding out your values will help you to find your life purpose, your fulfilment, it will help you in finding your motivation, your inner strength and will make you work much harder towards your goals.

There is a general belief that all women value family and relationships more than a career satisfaction. This type of thinking can lead to many commonly experienced issues like: poor life satisfaction, poor work life balance, or even low mood or depression. Unfortunately not many of us know themselves very well. We women don't often have the luxury to take time to get to know ourselves. Quite often we find out what we don't want, before we find out what we do want. The best example of that is our relationships, including our romantic relationships. Only by living with someone, under the same roof and having them regularly present in your life, you will learn what aspects of their behaviour irritate you and which aspects are you happy with. I have some female friends who are very fulfilled in their primary role of a caregiver and a family maker. I know few women who want to be businesswoman first and a mum second, and those who do, are the happiest at work and would never swap the order of their priorities and put their family first. It's important that you get to know yourself and empower yourself to live your life according to yours, and not somebody else's values.

Don't ever swap the priorities of your values to suit someone else's expectations. Knowing this about yourself will help you improve your relationships, will help you communicate more effectively and or build a more successful business. You might have found that one of your highest values is wealth building or equally you might find that being healthy and staying healthy is most important to you. Knowing your highest values might also help you to decide that you want to have a greater social impact on the lives of other people, and giving back to the community matters to you more than being wealthy. You need to find your authentic self and live according to your highest values. Don't give into the pressure of living in a certain way that society or a family might put on you. Many of us were raised in traditional families, it's worth to bear in mind that this might have impacted our current values system.

The areas of your life where you're not empowered in - other people are going to overpower you. This is almost a given. You might get distracted by ideas of other people who will impact how you live your life or how you enjoy your life and how you're making decisions or how you spend your free time. You need to strive to be empowered in as many areas of your life as possible to be free.

Dr John Demartini, author and professional speaker says *"It's very important to fill your day with high priority actions, so you don't fill your day with low priority distractions"*. Ladies, this message is for you - only by knowing your highest values you are able to live your life freely, in an authentic way, focusing on what you really love. This is why you should never judge yourself or others for having different values. Your highest values could be: having a balanced life, being healthy, having a good physical appearance. It could be power and status, social impact, wealth building, creating legacy for your children, or positive and fulfilling relationships.

There are many different ways in which you can find out what your highest values are. Please check our suggestions at the end of this book. However, an easy way to figure out what is important to you is by practising self awareness and observing your reactions in certain life situations: for example during a heated discussion when you don't feel heard or understood, perhaps when you feel ignored or disrespected, you might have a really strong reaction that "came out of the blue". Learn what is important to you by the way you react, in the absence of what you want. Be kind and gentle to yourself. Be your best friend.

## 2

# The Power of Your Mind

In this chapter we will talk about your mind and what makes it the most powerful tool you have at your disposal. Your brain is your creative servant. It is there to help you create your future experiences. The brain is a mechanism wired to expect that what you anticipate will come true. It's almost like your brain is invested in helping you prepare for the arrival of what you expect, not of what you want.

Your brain will help you generate thoughts and solutions you would never have believed would come up to you. If you expect to find a good job, then your brain will start to generate ideas how to make it happen. If you don't expect it, then your brain will not do this work. It is not as simple as *you want a new job*. You have to literally expect and believe that you will find a better job in order for the brain to come up with a way to make that happen.

That expectation and belief are crucial factors here. Many people go through their lives wanting lots of things but never believing they can really have them, so their minds never work on ways to bring those things about. As a result what they want never shows up. You need to expect it and believe it to make it happen. This dynamic relates to the idea that we only act on what we believe to be true. Your brain would not work on helping you come up with solutions to things you didn't really expect. That would be a waste of its resources. Changing what we anticipate starts with what we think. However, as we just discussed, our language-based thinking makes up only a small part of the mind's processing ability. To really use the full power of your mind to change expectations, you need to use sensory based images as well as activate deeper, faster levels of processing. Your first visualisation of something is like a switch in your brain. When it is turned on, it triggers the brain to generate a solution or a way to obtain what you are expecting. It's unfortunate that so many people are so limited in their beliefs about what they can get that what they want will never flip that switch and will never show up.

These limiting beliefs are holding us back and this is why it is so vital to just think about the presence of what you want, instead of the absence of it. When you think of the presence of what you want, your brain automatically starts to create that first visual image that flips the switch. It turns on your mind as a solution generating process. Those visual images can really work to our advantage.

As you begin to shift your expectations and to actively direct your thoughts towards what you want, things you never noticed before in your environment will show up and start assisting you in achieving your goal. This is quite interesting because what happens sometimes is that - for example, when we buy a new car, suddenly we see the same car driving everywhere. If we activate an image after a little while we prime our brain to selectively notice those things that match up with this image.

As we know, there is far more happening in our environment that we could possibly pay attention to. When you start to focus on something specifically, the brain selectively shifts its attention to finding the things in the environment that match up with what you are thinking about. This is why people with depression often notice negative things in their environment and happier people notice things to feel happy about. The pattern then feeds itself. If you see depressing things, you feel more depressed, and then you will look for more depressing things. We all live with an illusion that we are aware of what is happening around us, but the reality is that we have a limited attention capacity, which allows us to see a small amount of what is going on around us.

So we only notice only the things we prime our brain to see by our expectations and our beliefs. Few people are active participants in creating what they see in the world and what they experience every day. But, this is something we can all achieve and this is something we should all work on. I encourage you to work on this part.

You can prime your brain using visualisations to start attracting the things you really want, the things you want to have, the places you want to go to, and goals you want to achieve and your brain will work its magic to create solutions to bring those things closer to you.

Please have a look at our exercises at the end of this book to understand more about how to use visualisations to help you achieve your goals.

<u>3</u>

## Challenge Your Beliefs

In this chapter we will talk about your belief system. We will discuss how your beliefs can hold you back and what you can do to challenge them and create new supportive beliefs. But, what is a belief ? Belief is a thought that we keep thinking. It's a thought we regularly think. As we have over twenty thousand thoughts per day we also have a large number of beliefs. So how does it all work ? Well, our beliefs can support us or they can work against us. Most of our beliefs are formed based on our past experiences and thoughts related to those past experiences. They are stored in our subconscious mind and form our belief system.

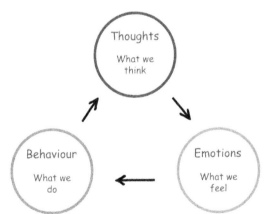

*Thoughts —> Events —> Feelings → Behaviour —> Beliefs*

In Cognitive Behavioural Therapy we usually focus on our current thoughts, our behaviours and relationships between thoughts and behaviour. We also focus on our moods and how we are feeling.

You could ask : *why do we have different thoughts about the same situations and why do we act differently under similar circumstances?* One of the main reasons for that is that we all have different sets of core beliefs. Core beliefs are our deeply held underlying beliefs that we have about ourselves, the world and people around us and they influence how we interpret our experiences, and that affects how we think, and how we act and engage with others.

Core beliefs are like tinted glasses through which we view things. Each one of us has a slightly different shade of tint (in some cases it can be vastly different). The basic aim of Cognitive Behavioural Therapy is to learn to change the way we think and act in order to change the way we feel. Core beliefs are important, because they determine how we think and act. If we change our core beliefs, changes in how we think and act will naturally follow, which will in turn help change the way we feel.

Not all core beliefs are negative. Let's look at some of our core beliefs because that way we will be able to understand them better. Negative core beliefs about ourselves can be grouped in three categories:

- *hopeless*
- *unlovable*
- *worthless*

For example, a hopeless core belief can be: *"I'm a failure"* or *"I'm a loser"*. An example of unlovable core belief could be: *"I'm unattractive"* or *"I don't fit in"*. Please have a look at the cheat sheet at the end of this book to see how those beliefs work and what could be applicable to you.

In between our core beliefs and our thoughts and behaviour there is also another level, which is called **Rules and Assumptions**. This is also called "intermediate beliefs" because they fall in between our core beliefs and our thoughts and behaviour. We can imagine the relationship between core beliefs, rules and assumptions and our thoughts and behaviour as if our mind was a tree. Core beliefs are the roots that anchor us and deliver water to the trunks. Branches are like rules and assumptions. The leaves are our thoughts and behaviour. We set up rules for ourselves for almost everything we do, which can be a dangerous thing. We often use statements like: *"I should", "I shouldn't", "I must", "I musn't"* or assumptions such as *"If .... something happens ... then ... something else will happen".*

For example if we have a core belief *"The world is a scary place"* we may have rules such as *"I must always keep myself and my family safe", "I shouldn't take any risks"* and assumptions such as *"If I'm not careful enough then something bad is going to happen to me". "If I relax too much then I'm going to get hurt"* - *"If I don't take any risks I will stay safe"*

As you can see these rules and assumptions can influence our behaviour because we act in ways that avoid violating our rules or avoid the negative consequences of our thoughts. We might avoid anything that we perceive as scary or something that provokes anxiety. This is also known commonly as self sabotage.

For example, If we want to start a business, as a woman we might think:

- *"Having a successful business is hard. I will never be able to combine it with family life"*
- *"If I have a successful business then I will definitely neglect my family".*

That is an untrue statement but that is also a negative belief that is working against us. It's important to recognise that our negative beliefs, assumptions and rules, according to which we live, form the basis for our behaviour. Creating new beliefs, however, can truly transform your life. If we want to understand ourselves better, it's worth asking a question: *"What's going through my head right now?"* That question usually works. That's because no matter what we're going through at any given moment in life, we usually are able to take a step back and notice what we are thinking. But if I ask you what are your core beliefs, what rules do you live by, and what assumptions do you make about yourself, the world and other people, you will probably not know where to look for an answer and the answer might not come straight away. Our core beliefs develop over time beginning in our childhood, with lessons we learn from our parents and things we learn through observation, as well as things we've learnt from our interactions with other people, such as siblings, relatives, teachers, role models, friends, and peers. This is when our beliefs are formed and one way to uncover core beliefs is you can simply ask yourself :

- *What did I learn from my parents?*
- *What did I learn from my family?*
- *What did I learn about myself, about the world and other people?*
- *Did I form any beliefs?*
- *Did I form any rules or assumptions based on what I learned from my parents?*

Take a sheet of paper and make a list, answer those questions. You can also have a look at the exercises at the end of this book and examine your beliefs further. Examine what role people play in your current belief system?

Core beliefs develop as a result of the experiences we have as children so think of your early life experiences and ask yourself:

- *What did I learn from my family and friends about myself, about the world and about other people?*
- *Did I form any negative beliefs?*
- *And are these beliefs holding me back in my life today?*

Also it's worth having a look at or making a list of people who have been influential in your life throughout your whole life span and other significant experiences you've had since your childhood and try to explore how those people and experiences influence your core belief system. This is the first step and it will help you uncover what beliefs you have. The next step is to create new supporting beliefs.

## 4

## Your Relationships

Although very few admit it, motherhood can be a tough journey through an unknown territory. Sadly, many women lose themselves in the process of becoming a mother and a caretaker. Many of us are raised in a traditional way, believing that if we put the needs of other people above our own needs, our relationships will be a source of joy and happiness. However, this rarely happens.

Most mums get stuck somewhere between their own biology, societal pressure and a culture that still idealises motherhood full of sacrifice. When they finally give birth they try at all costs to be their own version of a *"perfect mother"*. The mother that has everything under her control, is patiently accepting everything coming her way and doesn't need anything else to be happy.

In contrast to this *"perfect mother"* there is a mother who is *"good enough"*. She understands the needs of her child but doesn't give up on herself. She doesn't neglect her relationships, her dreams or plans. Being a mother she still is a woman, a friend and a wife. She might be tired, lost and emotional at times, but she cares for her baby the best she can. She is focused on that, not the version of being the *"perfect"* mother. She still believes in love and romantic love plays a big role in her life. However, as we know love means different things to different people. We all want it and need it. We love that warm feeling inside love gives us. When love is present in our lives we feel happy, content and positive - like nothing seems impossible. When it's missing we feel lost and vulnerable. But does it have to be so black and white? Is it possible to find your sweet spot and stay there? How do we stay more balanced and less affected when our relationship circumstances change? The answer is : Yes, it is possible! Here are our few ideas on how to get there:

**1. Love yourself first**
As we go through life we don't often have time to get to know ourselves. Our dreams, fears and desires often come to the surface only in situations where we are being tested by life. We become so much wiser later in life. Once we know ourselves, it's much easier to understand our partner and the dynamics of our relationships. One way to become happier in life is to love and be kind to yourself. Don't forget who you really are and don't give up your interests, hobbies and friends. If you do, your dreams will come back and haunt you, reminding you of what is important.

**2. Work on yourself and remain attractive for your partner**
The most important relationship you can build in your life is the one you have with yourself. There is unlimited love, power and strength inside you. You just need to learn how to access it. It's completely achievable. Once you tap into your inner power you can build the most joyful, happy and balanced connection with your partner - one where you are both independently fulfilled and happy. You will enjoy contributing to each other's lives instead of over relying on each other. That's when magic happens.

**3. Learn to communicate effectively**
Sometimes, when you have been together for a while you might feel like things are becoming a bit stale and you start drifting apart. It's natural and most people feel like that. The excitement that was present at the early stage of your relationship is gone and reality kicks in. This could make you feel disappointed, discouraged or sad. The warm, fuzzy feeling of being in love is gone. That's when most couples come to terms with the fact it will take some work. Open and honest communication is what can prevent painful arguments. Remember that nobody is a mind reader. It's your job to express your feelings, fears and expectations. It's not your partner's job to guess them, despite the "mystical connection" that you believe the two of you might have. So explain how your partner's behaviour makes you feel. Communicate how you want things to

change. Be calm, patient and positive and believe that he or she can change. Try your best not to judge or criticise.

### 4. Keep things fresh and fun
Find time to do fun things with and without your partner. Never neglect this part. Make time to go out as a couple. Dress nicely and make an effort. Go to new places, make new friends, get a new hobby or improve on your current one. You need to stay fresh and attractive for yourself and your partner. Just because you are a mum doesn't mean that you should ignore this part. Invest in yourself and in your relationship. The results will be visible in your confidence levels and in your wellbeing. Your work results will improve too. Your partner will find you more attractive, you will find yourself more attractive. And they might even be more inclined to follow the same path and work on themselves.

### 5. Change your mindset = Change your life
We humans associate certain experiences and situations with positive and negative memories from our past. Our thoughts and emotions form patterns of our behaviour. The longer we live the more established these patterns become. Our thinking creates our mood and our mood creates our mindset. This is why it's so important to think positively as a negative mindset can hold us back from living a happy life. So, in order to form new positive thoughts patterns try thinking differently about your partner and your relationship. Learn about common causes of issues between couples. Learn how relationships function and the differences between men and women. Instead of complaining or demanding an instant improvement in your partner, include some logic and a bit of a scientific approach to your life. This will open your heart to experience more love.

### 6. Don't be shy and ask for help
Life can be hard at times. Nobody is immune to work stress, lack of sleep or the pressure you are under when your child is ill. You are not a superhero and neither is your partner. The sooner you accept it the better for you. Don't sit and complain about how tough you've got it. Think about practical solutions. Can you drop off the kids to your mum's and finish your work? Can you book a nanny and go out with your husband? Learn to meditate to sleep better or

perhaps read something informative or funny to make your work commute less stressful? These minor adjustments can make a huge difference to the quality of our everyday life and our relationship.

Many women are yet to learn the art of prioritising their own needs and acting on their desires. Many women are yet to learn self-confidence and standing their ground. Motherhood is a journey that has many learning curves. It requires a woman to be kind and gentle with herself. To show herself love and care, and once she learns the art of self-love and self-care, her relationships begin to flourish..

## 5

# Selecting Your Tribe

In this chapter we will discuss how to select your tribe, your supporters, and people who will help you grow and develop. We will also discuss the connection of your self-esteem and self-worth to selecting the right people and associating and surrounding yourself with the right people in your life.

To some of you, the concept of self-worth is already familiar. Self-worth is our inner image. It's the way in which we perceive ourselves and our life. There is a general self-worth, which is stable and does not change much. This is the way in which we see ourselves. That general self-worth does not depend on external conditions or external goods. There is also relative self-worth, which is based on how we feel when somebody gives us a compliment or how we feel when we buy an expensive car.

You might wonder where does self-worth come from? It comes from our childhood and people who are around us. Ever since we are small we hear from others: who we are, how we are. Family has a crucial impact on how we perceive ourselves from a young age. The level of self acceptance and self-worth is mostly formed during our childhood. We have certain mechanisms which we use to feel better about who we are, for example: treating ourselves to a nice meal, a night out or buying a gift. It's worth to remember that self-worth, however, has nothing to do with those external things. It's more connected with seeing yourselves in a positive light for who you are, not what you have. People sometimes increase their self-worth by associating themselves with groups of other people who can make them feel better, but this isn't sustainable in the long term. It isn't a healthy way to increase your self-esteem. We need to work on feeling good about ourselves despite how others see us and feel about us. Practising this will give us a high level of self-esteem, which in return will give us an opportunity for emotional freedom.

It's a freedom to choose when to react, how to express yourselves, who to be friends with, and how to live your life. So that we are not dependent on the opinions of others, we don't rely on the fact that somebody likes us or not. We feel good regardless. We need to cultivate this positive self image and positive self-esteem in us because from that we will get emotional freedom. This freedom is very valuable and it's hugely connected to people we are actually spending our time with. I don't mean here our husbands or our children but external people like friends, acquaintances or contacts. These people are very connected to the level of our self-esteem and self-worth.

It's important to notice that people with low self-esteem are very sensitive to how others see them. They take everything to heart, it's very easy to hurt them. They are quite often unhappy about who they are. They get obsessed with their self image and they might get obsessed with what others think of them.

People with low self esteem quite often don't accept themselves for who they are and they don't really like themselves. So what they often do is they are looking to surround themselves with people who will make them feel good, who will boost their confidence, give them a compliment and give them that approval that they are really hungry for. This is not something we should be doing on the long-term basis.

We should be basing our decision who to spend time with, on our common interests, our goals, our hobbies and what we want to achieve in life, not based on who is going to give me their approval. Let's work on positive self-esteem and build a network of people that can support us in our growth. Our friendships are often a reflection of our positive self image. This is because hanging out in the environment that supports us is very different to spending time with people just to get their approval. If we spend time with people who perhaps are not very confident themselves, they are unlikely to give us encouraging advice and show optimism to our latest business idea. A friend is someone who should be able to give you constructive feedback guilt free, regardless of how that feedback makes you feel, and knowing that you are not going to dump them as a friend. A friend is not someone who should shower you with compliments and make you feel good about who you are at all times. If someone is telling you that you are doing everything great, they are not giving you a platform to grow. We often spend time with people who are likely to give us a compliment, likely to be similar to us, have similar struggles and often by sharing your struggles, with them or vice versa, we feel a little bit better for a while. But that is not something I recommend doing in the long term.

What I recommend is building a positive self-image and a good level of self-esteem. This is step one. This takes time and practice. Step two is setting goals, deciding what I want to achieve, for example:

- *Do I want to stay the same or do I want to change my life?*
- *And what types of things do I want to change?*

Step three is writing down:

- *How does my current circle of friends support me in my goals, in the goals that I want to achieve, in the plans I want to make reality?*
- *How do current people who are present in my life support me in that?*

Step four is connecting with people who have similar goals, strive for similar things, or perhaps have already succeeded in this. If you don't know anyone like that then look at your current circle of friends and write down who is most likely to support you and who is less likely to support you?

- *who makes you feel good when you're discussing your future plans ?*
- *who is interested in your future plans and who makes you feel doubtful about your skills and abilities, or perhaps make you feel confused or low by regularly transferring their anxiety on you?*

During this process you might realise that you spend lots of time with people who don't support you the way they should or they show you no interest in your future plans. Remember at the end of the day we are the average of 5 people we spend most time with! Let's build positive self esteem so that we don't continuously look for approval or advice on what to do.

A positive self image will tell us what is best for us, will make us trust ourselves and we will know when to take action. If we continuously look for advice and opinions of others whether we should take a new direction in life, whether we should change our job, and so on, they will advise us what to do from their point of view i.e: ***what is best for them, not what is the best for us***. This is because they see the world from their perspective, not your perspective. Only we know what's best for us and what makes us really happy and what to change. Other people will not understand the significance of this even if we explain this to them. So, it's all nice and supportive to share our struggles with others, as long as this does not consume all of our energy.

If you really want to improve your life, if you are looking for a change, a better life satisfaction, be selective about who you are spending your time with.

Ask yourself a question:

- ***Are you happy to be the average of the five people you spend most time with or do you want something different?***

## 6

# Does Your Mental Health Affect Your Children?

Welcome to chapter six. In this chapter we will discuss how your mental health affects your children and what you can do to change it.

Parenthood is not easy at the best of times. Parents can often feel overwhelmed and stressed out and can really struggle with staying balanced and calm. And this affects all of us really but unfortunately, to our disadvantage, children very often pick up on our emotions. And whether we like it or not – it does affect them! Loving relationships with responsible adults are essential to children's healthy development and while most parents are very aware of children's physical growth, the bond with their child has also got a huge influence on their brain development. So, for example, by the age five, a child's brain is about 90% developed. And children's relationships with adults are the key to healthy life as they set out the foundation of their emotional maturing. Children learn to experience emotions, express them, and relate to others.. among many other things, mostly from their parents. During early years, as we know, they can also go through mental health problems. However, quite often these issues are not addressed as quickly as they can be or even taken seriously.

So, when children face traumatic events such as emotional distress, parents' divorce, parents' arguments or death in the family or house move, it threatens their mental health. We use the term Adverse Childhood Experiences (ACEs) to describe these traumatic events. Family financial problems are one of the most common one followed by divorce or separation of a parent or a guardian. Other common adverse experiences that can affect your kids could be:

- *Poverty or homelessness*
- *Chronic neglect*
- *Being a victim of domestic abuse*
- *Parent's poor mental illness*
- *Separation of parents or divorce*
- *Families with high conflict (for example, regular arguments between parents)*
- *Racism or violence*

The impact of chronic neglect, violence, or parental mental illness has lifelong implications on every child. It puts children at a high risk of developing mental health disorders among other things. They are more prone to addictions in the future, it impacts their physical health. And it reinforces their negative self-image, which then further has a negative impact on their confidence and their academic results.

We know that all families experience challenges but how you deal with them means everything. Quite often the pressure is on the mum to keep peace between her and her partner. Challenges in the families don't necessarily mean that the emotional development of children will suffer. Many parents with mental health problems manage their condition, and their children do not experience any adverse effects. Many children will grow up with a parent who might have a mild form of mental illness. When parents have access to support, they can really minimise the impact their illness or their stress levels have on their children.

I think it's important to take note that we all face stress, we all face relationship difficulties, we all face different levels of financial pressure or poor work life balance, but it's noticing that when these things have a big impact on who we become over time, how we speak, how we perceive ourselves, how we talk to our children, how we talk to our partner, do we allow enough time for selfcare?

These are the questions we need to be asking ourselves and recognizing how regular stress has on our day to day lives, the life that our children observe and are part of. Because it's the negative habits that impact our children the most.

**What Can You Do to Support Your Family's Mental Wellbeing?**

Well, first of all - don't let stigma prevent you from seeking help. So, be honest about mental health issues. Be honest with yourself and with your family about your perhaps difficulties to handle stress and pressure at work. Be honest about it. Don't be afraid to open up and speak about it. Acknowledging your difficulties is step one for your recovery. Some parents do not want to talk about this with their kids, but kids are much smarter than we think so they will pick up on our emotions and our behaviour anyway. If we don't openly talk to them about it they will often misinterpret our behaviour and our actions and take it really against themselves and start blaming themselves for it. By discussing mental health with your family, children can be taking a supportive part in your recovery process.

Other things you can do to empower your kids are:

- *Actively listen to them*
- *Provide a safe and open home environment, where your kids, yourself and your partner can be who you are, can stay true to yourself.*
- *Avoid labels such as "depressed" or "anxious" as they may be too foreign for your child to use. Instead you could use words like "sad" and "scared"*
- *Let your child express their emotions at all times and talk about them with you*
- *Try to build strong relationship with your child where you both open up to your weaknesses and you acknowledge them*
- *Always try to model healthy behaviour as much as you can*

Building this close relationship with your child where they can tell you when something is going wrong and you can tell them when something is going wrong. It's a little bit like a partnership. Many of us think that because our child is our child, it belongs to us and it should do as we tell them to, and they should follow all our instructions and not step out of the line. It should just be there to listen to us. But everyone has independent character and personality and children are capable of their own thinking and using their own brain in creative ways. So, we need to acknowledge that our children are intelligent and they deserve to know the truth.

If you want your children to behave in a certain way or build confidence, build a positive self-image, you need to really model this behaviour. If you want them to express sadness or tell you when something is going wrong at school, for example, then you should be telling them when something's going wrong for you at work. Perhaps not to a great detail but sharing what's going on.

- Trying to stay calm during arguments or heated family discussions is very important. Raising your voice rarely helps anybody. It's really important no matter what the argument is about with your partner or with your child to really stay calm. You are very likely to get much better results because you are staying calm and collected even if it is something you are really upset about.

- Giving your children hugs and showing that you love them every day no matter what you are facing in terms of your own mental health is super important. They need to know that you have their back. They need to know that you love them and you will protect them no matter what. That will give them strength and confidence.

- Teaching effective communication and coping skills is one of the things that your children don't learn at school. So, the only way they can really learn how to communicate and cope with difficult situations in life is from you, your partner and your family. So, just bear that in mind that when they go to school, they will not learn how to respond to bullies or they will not learn how to manage exam stress. You are there for that purpose and you need to pick up that responsibility and teach that to your kids.

- Encouraging your partner to support "no mental health stigma" at home is also crucial. That no stigma environment will promote openness between you and your child and it will really strengthen your relationship.

- Learn how to better manage emotions and reduce your stress. Try to cultivate self-care and remember to take time off to relax and unwind. That will impact the state of your mental health and it will positively impact your relationship with your children. So, cultivating self-care and taking time to relax and unwind is very important to everyone even if that means half an hour per week. That's much better than nothing.

Making quality time for your partner, doing something fun together is equally important. So, do not neglect your relationship with your partner because that will have a negative impact on your mental health and therefore the mental health of your children. It will indirectly affect the mental health of your children. Your children will feel the difference when you are calm and relaxed. They will see that in the way you communicate with them, in the way you are around them. So, you need to remember about self-care and you need to remember about finding time for your partner and finding time to do something romantic and something fun together. Also, do your best to create a safe home environment and work on improving your relationships with others.

Try different things and more importantly don't be shy to look for external resources and professional help if you feel your mental health is affecting you or your family. It's very important to reach out and ask for help. And if you don't feel convinced that's what you need, do it for the sake of your children, because they are counting on a stable and secure and safe home environment, so you owe this to them. Don't be afraid to look for help. Don't be afraid to educate yourself on this topic

## 7

# **Managing Stress**

When two individuals, with different family backgrounds decide to live together under the same roof, there are bound to be some changes. Relationships, to be successful, require a series of adjustments by both partners. Things usually have a smooth start when a couple first gets together. People are generally good at handling their differences. However, things tend to change when two people get married or decide to start a family together. New and unfamiliar circumstances can increase uncertainty and cause anxiety, which needs to be managed in the right way, for a relationship to survive.

There will be times when there will be differences. Most of them are ignored, especially at the beginning of a relationship. However, when the other pressures appear, like a new job, a new baby or a house move, suppression of these differences, cannot be maintained. New and unfamiliar circumstances increase anxiety.

It may surprise you to know that the highest rates of distress are found in married women. Studies have shown that, in general, employment has a positive effect on the mental health of women by improving economic status, increasing their self-esteem and social contact and elevating boredom. Historically speaking, men hold power and authority and women are rewarded for such psychological traits as submissiveness, compliance, helplessness which accommodate and please men. Modern women are struggling to break away from this traditional role and to find new rules of independence and personal growth that raise their self-esteem.

Such struggles consume energy and leave them feeling drained. Even if a woman is not physically overworked, boredom, low self-esteem and inner turmoil frustrate her and drop her off all her creative energy. So what is the answer? Surely not to choose between family or career? The life consisting of all family and no work or no family and all work, is an unbalanced life. We need both love and work in a harmonious proportion which boosts our energy and happiness and makes us healthy and productive. When feelings are oppressed in a relationship they lead to chronic resentment. Standing up for your rights might be useful when dealing with injustice at work but being over assertive in a relationship can cause unnecessary conflict. Long hidden conflicts lead to more stress and many psychosomatic diseases.

## *Divorce or Separation*

In terms of stress score, divorce ranks second only to bereavement according to Holms and Rahe Life Events Score. The ease with which a divorce can be obtained can lead to the destabilisation of the marriage and the break up. It is unlikely that a divorce can be free of tension, conflict, sadness, regrets or pain. Before accepting that the marriage is over, there is a face of disbelief that this could happen. Partners are likely to alternate between hope and despair. Relationships with family and friends have to be renegotiated on the basis of new social identity, financial proportion has to be made, and most painful of all order implications for the children. A lot of adjustment is needed before the feeling of loss and emptiness can give away to the new meaning of life. It has been suggested that after bereavement such an adjustment takes two years. After a divorce it takes five. The reason for such a long drawn out period is the continuing attachment to and sense of connectedness with a former partner which prevents the establishment of a new life. The legal process of divorce can also be emotionally draining. Being preoccupied by their own hurt ego and insecurity, partners may forget that their conflict can seriously affect their children and behave like children themselves. Sometimes disputes are deliberately prolonged in order to avoid facing grief and emptiness or communicating the news to the children. However, children are extremely perceptive and leaving them out of the dispute when they already have a sense the world is falling apart can be very stressful to them. Some children handle signs of separation relatively easily while others show severe behavioural disturbances. Their school performance may drop and they might become unmotivated, anxious or depressed.

Some children will try very hard for their parents to stay together. The children suffering is likely to further increase the stress on a couple. Divorce or separation of parents is undoubtedly a traumatic event for children and they will need reassurance and love from both parents. They are likely to cope better if the relationship between the ex-partners remains amicable and if they are not required to take the side of mum or dad. It's usually only with professional help, strong support from friends and relatives, and determination to overcome the pain and anger by expressing their emotions that children and adults learn to live "normally" again.

### *Attitudes and Beliefs*

Not everyone responds to a potentially stressful situation in the same way. The simple reason is that it is not the outside stressor alone that is important, but also how we interact with that stressor. We often have unrealistic and very high expectations. If we expect to win every contract, pass every exam, please every person or never make mistakes, we are demanding such perfect standards that we are bound to disappoint ourselves. Psychiatrists say that most fatigue stems from our mental and emotional attitudes. Emotions which drain us of energy and lack of joy and contentment. We rarely get tired when we do things which are interesting and exciting for us. As we grow up our beliefs are generated or modified by the need to win approval from peers and the need to belong to a group. To ensure peer acceptance, we learn to live by the rules and beliefs of the peer group regarding how to handle many various life situations.

In summary, most beliefs and rules are formed in response to our needs and our past experiences. We have learned them from our parents and peers and from our need to feel good about ourselves, and from our need to be loved and belong and feel safe. They have nothing to do with truth or reality, but the power of beliefs is such that we accept them as absolute truth, not just for us but for everybody in the world, which can be very destructive.

There is a lot you can do to minimise the impact stress has on you and your family. Please have a look at our exercises, cheat sheets and suggestions to learn more on how to manage stress.

## 8

## Developing a Kind Inner Voice

In this chapter we will discuss the power of your voice and how to develop a kinder inner voice to better serve you in your daily life and in your future goals.

The most important words are the words you say to yourself when others don't listen. Much of our stress is due to silent conversations we have with ourselves. Psychologists call this a negative self-talk. We talk ourselves into the ground by programming ourselves negatively. Negative self talk services in our attitudes, beliefs, expectations, interpretations and predictions.

When we blow things out of proportion by using words like *"extremely"*, *"incredibly"*, *"always"* or *"never"* we often come to believe in the things we repeat to ourselves. The tendency to put ourselves down is self-destructive. In fact, self-esteem and vulnerability are inversely related: when self-esteem is high - vulnerability is low and vice versa. Some people call this critical inner voice. Everyone has a critical inner voice including you, but people with low self-esteem have a particularly vicious one. It calls us names like *"stupid"* or *"lazy"* whenever we make the slightest mistake. Our voice compares us with other people and their successes and it tells us that we will never achieve *"that"* because we are not capable. If we are any less than perfect we are nothing. Our inner voice exaggerates our weak points and dismisses our strengths.

Why do we listen to this critical inner voice? We listen to it because it makes us feel safe and by raising our defences it prepares us for a possible defeat in the future. If we have an adequate amount of self-esteem it will help us confront challenges and solve problems instead of worrying about them, often before they appear. More often than not our inner voice really undermines our self-worth. Another reason why the critical voice has such a strong hold on us is that there is a part of us that is willing to believe that its approval, just like one of our parents, is necessary for our survival…Negative thinking in adults and in children is linked to poor health because of our thoughts which determine our behaviour. Critical inner voice and poor self image often leads to a feeling of helplessness, which turns into helpless behaviour and even depression.

The power of your inner voice is huge! We and our children are capable of more things when our inner voice is kind and supportive rather than harsh and demanding. Did you know that when our inner voice is harsh and critical we have the same reaction as if we were arguing with someone and wanted to run away? When we are not speaking kindly to ourselves, when we are harsh about something (that we just did or just happened) - at that point in our body our cortisol level goes up and we don't want to do anything. The only thing we can think of is fight or run away. So this type of voice is not putting us in a frame of mind where we are motivated to do any work or improve anything. It's an important fact and it's worth bearing that in mind.

- *What do you think about your inner voice?*
- *How do you speak to yourself when nobody listens?*
- *Is your voice likely to be gentle and supportive ? OR*
- *Does it sound really harsh when something doesn't go to plan?*

Pay attention to how you talk to yourself, how you talk about yourself, your skills, your dreams and your plans. How does the tone of your voice sound? It's really important to take control of our inner critic, because we are capable of much more when our voice is kind and supportive, rather than strong and demanding. Adults and kids who have low self-esteem often think that others don't think of them in a positive light. They think that even when they have no proof of that. So the low self-esteem and this inner critic goes very much hand-in-hand. The moment our voice becomes kinder and softer and more encouraging our self-esteem goes up and so does our confidence. So always try to speak to yourself as if you were speaking to your best friend. There is a very little chance, when you speak to yourself like that, that you will fail or become lazy. There is a very high chance however that, when you develop a kind voice, you will succeed in whatever is that you are doing.

## 9

## Becoming Your Best Friend

Welcome to chapter nine. In this chapter we will talk about the importance of becoming your best friend. I will explain why this is so important and how it can help you in the long term.

In a world where we constantly strive to prove ourselves and gain approval from others, it's very important to become your best friend. Relying on others for the feeling of self-worth and acceptance can be only effective in the short term. Sadly most of us don't know about it. This is not something we learn at school and it's not a social norm to learn that accepting yourself for who you are, and finding positive characteristics in yourself will be the key to forming healthy relationships with others. However, it's safe to say that we can't love others unless we love ourselves. This becomes even more important when trying to introduce changes to your life.

As you know we are all social animals. We naturally want to be part of a community and by association with others raise our chances for a better life. Being social animals we crave the approval of others, we want to connect with others. We join groups to feel noticed, to feel acknowledged and to be heard. This is all fine as long as we are not relying on others when trying to transform any aspect of our life. We women need to learn how to accept ourselves for who we are and not be so self critical. We need to acknowledge the positive aspects in us and build on them. This sounds easier than it is in reality but we need to practise self-acceptance, self-care, and self-awareness. By practising these things we will be moving closer to developing self confidence and becoming our own best friend. You have reached out for this book for a reason. You want something different, something better and more fulfilling in your life. You are totally capable of getting there, but the key thing is that you hold yourself accountable for the changes you make in your life and the goals you're setting.

We mums are so busy with daily responsibilities, we often lack time for ourselves. Yet, finding time for ourselves is the most important thing we should do. So start small. Find 5 minutes at the end of the day to be still and gentle with yourself. Do whatever makes you happy, but show yourself love. The love that perhaps not many other people are showing you. Be your best friend. You are in charge of your life. So start practising self acceptance and self love. This will increase your self worth, your self esteem and give you confidence and a feeling of control in your life. Small changes can make a big difference. Creating new habits: like going to sleep earlier to help you restore your body and mind and have a fresh outlook on life the next day is a great idea. It might allow you to have a morning coffee in the garden when your children are still asleep or go for a walk with a dog and enjoy the silence around you. Do whatever you desire but make time for self-care and self-love.

Many of us are in not very happy relationships or marriages. This is the reality. For most of us life didn't turn out to be the way we were hoping. But, it's never too late to change it. We women are very resilient, we are strong, and we are in charge of so many things in our families and our communities. Yet, we often lack connection with ourselves. You have the opportunity to change it now. Be in charge of your relationship with yourself. Reconnect with yourself, your dreams and your life goals. Start building this connection with yourself by being still and the sooner you will start practising it, the sooner positive change will happen in your life. When there is no noise around you, you will be able to build a positive inner voice which is crucial to becoming your best friend. Practise self acceptance and develop a supportive inner voice. This will help you in creating the basis of a positive change in your life..

Have a look at some suggestions at the end of this book to get a better idea on how to become your own best friend.

## 10

## Focus on Your Future

In this chapter we will talk about your future. We will discuss taking responsibility for your actions and we will discuss self-discipline and what role self-discipline plays in creating your dream life.

Let's start with talking about responsibility. Taking responsibility for changing your life is a big one. It can sound a little intimidating but it doesn't have to be. It's important to point out that only people who have a high level of self-esteem are able to take responsibility for their lives. This is because in order to take responsibility we need to trust ourselves first. We trust ourselves generally more when we know our self-worth. So that's when we know we can succeed at something, we will manage something, no matter what life throws at us. Building this self-worth is really important, a self-worth that does not depend on external goods, on what we have and depends on how we feel about ourselves internally, no matter what we have.

When we don't trust ourselves we struggle to take responsibility for our actions and our lives. People with low self-worth often take responsibility for the lives of others - for example they get involved in helping others by offering their time, offering their advice, even when it's not needed. They do that to take away the focus from changing their own life which is something they are deeply scared of.

People get involved in the lives of others because they can't get something they very much need - and that's the feeling of self-worth. They would often look for approval from others because that's their way of feeling good about themselves. Because they help someone, they're being valuable to someone, but it can be quite irritating if we are on the other side - if we are the other person, who perhaps is not looking for help or advice. Instead of giving our unsolicited help and advice we should be focusing on building the feeling of self-worth internally so we don't have to rely on others to make us feel good about who we are.

When there are no people to help, when nobody needs us anymore, if we have a low level of self-esteem, we suddenly feel terrible about ourselves. Nobody appreciates us, nobody values us, nobody needs our help and because we don't value ourselves we are feeling completely empty inside. Relying on others to feel good is not the way to do it. Looking for approval externally can be very dangerous and it's never a long-term solution.

This type of internal sabotage can be quite hard to notice at times. Sometimes we are setting ourselves up to fail just to prove to ourselves that we are not great at something. People with low self-esteem often do that. They would create opportunities to prove to themselves that they are not good at something, that they can't do it. Something like *"See, I told you I would never succeed at that"* and they can give up quite easily and quickly. Taking responsibility for your life also means taking action so doing something to improve the situation. The more action we take the higher the likelihood is that we will succeed at something - which is often very connected to people with positive self image. These people can be very proactive. They are confident. They think positive things of themselves. They trust themselves and take action. They are really proactive, they realise that if there is a need to do something in their life they need to take action, instead of just talking about it, or dwelling on it, or discussing it with someone else.

People with high levels of self-esteem don't sit around and wait for things to happen but instead they take responsibility for their life in the sense that they learn from past mistakes so they don't give up that easily and they don't stop after one attempt. They look at what they've learned and they try something different and that proactiveness is a characteristic that we women need to really work on building internally. Looking for a solution and trying different approaches until something works. This is the way to do it. The work on our self-worth is a daily regular work; it's not something you build once and then you forget about it. It doesn't work that way. We need to cultivate the habit of working on our self-worth.

It's also important to remember that whatever we do, we should always focus on why we do it. What is the end result? What is the effect and what is the desired outcome are we looking for? For example, when we are trying to solve a problem, approaching a situation differently might be the right thing to do. Perhaps there was a conflict with a friend or with a partner and we've tried one approach, but it didn't work. Instead of giving up on that relationship we would be looking for a different approach, a different solution.

This is much better than going over and over, getting frustrated, talking about it, thinking about it and getting nowhere. Taking action and trying different approaches often works. And so is focusing on what we want, focusing on that end goal and end result. If we want to have a balanced life or perhaps to be more peaceful, let's bear that in mind when we are reacting and responding to different things, whether that is events or people.

Whenever you are not sure how to react you can stop yourself and ask yourself:

- *What is going through my head right now?*
- *What will make me more peaceful?*
- *What will make me more happy?*
- *Will continuing doing the same thing bring me closer to my desired outcome?*
- *Will responding to this situation bring me closer to my end result?*

People who see themselves in a positive light very often know exactly which way they are going and what desired outcome they are looking for. They might not know what life will look like in five years from now, but they know what next steps to take. This is important because quite often we are looking for excuses which prevents us from taking action, and changing our lives. Quite often we have a dream, we want to achieve something and we focus so much on the possible negative aspects of achieving that outcome and looking for excuses, that what we are doing is we are setting ourselves up to fail, before we even tried. This is not the way to do it. The way to do it is just taking the first step, and then taking the next step the next day. It's all about making a regular effort every day. It might be just dedicating 30 minutes a week to learn something new and then dedicating the next 30 minutes the week after. This step based approach will remove anxiety from your mind and will help us in achieving our desired goals.

Always keep your desired outcome in mind. The effects of these next steps will hardly be perfect. They will often be not perfect, but they are good enough to get us to the next level, few steps closer towards our goal. Taking responsibility for your life and taking responsibility for your actions is very closely connected to our feeling of self-worth and your positive self image. Work on that and make regular small changes.

## SUMMARY

Congratulations! You have now completed this book. I hope you found the information included here helpful and perhaps you are already using some of our tips in your daily life.

There are a couple of things I want to mention before we say official *goodbye*. First of all, lack of self care can really creep up on you and over time it can cause long term damage to your health and your relationships. Poor mental health is often one of the main reasons for depression, relationships breakdown and low life satisfaction. Secondly, we mums have a huge role to play in setting up examples for our children. Our kids observe us all the time. They learn by watching us and they store our behaviour as a model in their subconscious mind. So, remember to practise positive self-talk and display positive self image in front of your children as they are likely to listen and follow your footsteps. It's great that you've reached out for this book. I hope it will help you in understanding yourself and others better. I hope it will encourage you to take a more proactive role in improving your life.

Make sure you have a look at our suggestions and exercises provided at the end of this book. They will help you to put everything into context.

# ANNEX

## *EXERCISES*

Chapter 1   Knowing Your Values

Chapter 2   Creating Positive Expectations
            Creating Positive Experiences

Chapter 3   Recognising Our Core Beliefs
            Beliefs, Rules and Assumptions

Chapter 4   Loving Yourself First

Chapter 5   Your Support Network (part 1)
            Your Support Network (part 2)

Chapter 6   Supporting Your Mental Health

Chapter 7   Get to know your stressors

Chapter 8   Spotting Negative Phrases

Chapter 9   Practising Self-Acceptance
            Positive Future Self

Chapter 10  Celebrate Small Successes
            Focus On Your Future

# Chapter 1
## KNOWING YOUR VALUES

Living according to your highest value is crucial to a happy life. Do you know your value system? If not, answering questions below could be a good starting point.

1. Which aspect of your life brings you the most joy or satisfaction?

2. What would you like to spend more time on? (career, family, health, social impact, fitness, marriage, relaxing)

3. What 3 things (family, career, health, social impact, power&influence, marriage, fitness) are the most important to you?

4. Why are these things so important?

5. What can you do to start prioritise these values?

6. What actions can you take now to focus on your values?

Copyright 2022 VirtuallyThrive

# Chapter 2
## CREATING POSITIVE EXPECTATIONS

In the table below list your future events on the left site. Write down your current expection about this event on the right site of the table. Once that's done write a new more positive expectation below. This simple exercise allows you to take more proactive role in creating future experiences.

| List of events | Current & Future expectations |
| --- | --- |
| Example: Having a meeting with my manager at work | **Currently:** I feel anxious that my manager is going to be unpleasant again and speak to me with a patronising, rude tone. <br><br> **New expectation:** I feel a bit anxious about my meeting but this time I plan to prepare better and make this a constructive meeting where I'm more in charge. I'm sure it will turn out OK. |

# Chapter 2
## CREATING POSITIVE EXPERIENCES

Some people have hard time generating positive expectations and are always predicting worse case scenarios. Think about a future event that makes you anxious and ask yourself the questions below.

1. What is the possible negative outcome?

2. What is the likelihood that it would happen?

3. Has that ever happened to you before?

4. What would you like to happen instead?

5. How would it feel if your desired outcome came true?

6. What can you do to help the desired outcome come faster?

# Chapter 3
## RECOGNISING OUR CORE BELIEFS

Core beliefs define so many things in our mind. There are a number of ways that we can try to reveal our core beliefs and rules and assumptions.

Take a moment and complete the statements below:

" I am……."

" The world is……"

" Other people are……."

Do the same things with rules and assumptions. Complete the below sentences to help make you realise what rules you live by and think if they are serving you or not.

" I should……" "I should not…."

" I must ……." I must not….."

" If……….then….."

" If I ……….then……."

" If someone……then……"

Copyright 2022 VirtuallyThrive

# Chapter 3
## BELIEFS, RULES AND ASSUMPTIONS

Ask yourself who were the most influential people in your life starting from your childhood? What influence did they have on you and how you perceive the world today?

**What did you learn from these people about yourself, the world, and other people? Finish sentences below**

*I am ………..*

*The world is…………..*

*Others are………..*

**Did you form any rules or assumptions based on what you learned from these people?**

*I should/must ……..*

*I should not…………..*

*If I ……….(do this) ……then……..(this will happen) (etc.)*

*If I ……….(do this) ……then……..(other people will) (etc.)*

Copyright 2022 VirtuallyThrive

# Chapter 4
## LOVING YOURSELF FIRST

Loving yourself is the foundation for forming healthy relationships. In order to have healthy and happy relationships it's essential that you develop a supportive inner voice and practice self-acceptance and self love. Using examples below, write down 4 positive and encouraging affirmations about yourself.

Examples could be:
" I love and respect myself. I deserve love and respect from others"
" I am in charge of my future"
" I am fine the way I am. I am enough"

Your Positive Affirmations

1. ............................................................................................................
2. ............................................................................................................
3. ............................................................................................................
4. ............................................................................................................

Take note that repeating these affirmations out loud or in your head will help you develop your inner self-worth, self-confidence and a positive self image. It will also support you in creating coping skills and becoming more resilient.

Copyright 2022 VirtuallyThrive

# Chapter 5
## YOUR SUPPORT NETWORK

We need to focus on building a positive self esteem so that we don't continuously look for approval or advice on what to do. Positive self image will tell us what is good for us and what is not, and it will motivate us to take the steps necessary in achieving our goals.

The steps outlined below will help you in building a stronger support network

**STEP ONE**
The first step is about doing the hard work of creating a Positive Self-Image and cultivating a healthy level of self-esteem in us. This can be done by practising positive affirmations about yourself and finding regular time to do something you love. This stage is crucial in building our support network and it takes time and practice.

**STEP TWO**
Step two is about setting goals, deciding what I want and why. What is important to me and perhaps currently missing in my life? For example - Do I want to stay the same? Do I want change in my life and why? What aspects of my life am I not happy with?

**STEP THREE**
Step three is about writing down who is in my current support circle? (max 8 people) What are their names and their roles? Write down 3 ways in which each person supports you in your goals and in what you want to achieve in the future.

**STEP FOUR**
Step four is about who do I need to add to my support circle and why? What will their role be? Where can I find the right people and connect with them?

Copyright 2022 VirtuallyThrive

# Chapter 5
## YOUR SUPPORT NETWORK

We sometimes need to look at our network and decide who should stay in there and who should leave. There are different ways to do it, but one suggestion is to approach it as an exercise.

Using the table below write down on the left the names of people who support you the most and on the right hand-side names of people who support you the least. When writing down the names have a good think about who belongs to which column and why. Write down how much time you spend with people who support and how does this affect you? Should you perhaps limit how much time you spend with some people?

| MOST SUPPORT | LEAST SUPPORT |
|---|---|
|  |  |

Copyright 2022 VirtuallyThrive

# Chapter 6
## SUPPORTING YOUR MENTAL HEALTH

Please write down 3 most common situations where you struggle daily....

1.......

2.......

3.......

Write down 3 new things you are willing to try to improve your stress levels ...

1.......

2.......

3.......

# Chapter 7
## GET TO KNOW YOUR STRESSORS

Our stressors are part of our daily life. Using the table below, on the left handside highlight 4 most common stressors in your life. Then, using space on the right side write down 3 ways you will try to reduce the impact of this stressor on your life.

| Examples of Domestic Stressors | New Way of Approaching This |
|---|---|
| **Marriage**<br>• Lack of communication with spouse<br>• Recurrent financial problems<br>• Sexual difficulties leading to frustration<br>• High unmet expectations<br>• Different values and priorities leading to conflict<br>• Different sleeping patterns<br>• Irrational jealousy<br>• Unfaithfulness<br>• Sharing domestic chores<br>• Spouse smoking and drinking habits<br>• Spouse away from home too much<br>• Lack of compliments<br>• Illness of spouse<br>• Prolonged separation | |

Copyright 2022 VirtuallyThrive

# Chapter 7
## GET TO KNOW YOUR STRESSORS

Our stressors are part of our daily life. Using the table below, on the left handside highlight 4 most common stressors in your life. Then, using space on the right side write down 3 ways you will try to reduce the impact of this stressor on your life.

| Examples of Domestic Stressors | New Way of Approaching This |
|---|---|
| **Children**<br>- Sleep disturbances due to crying infant<br>- Disobedient children<br>- Jealous sibling<br>- Temper tantrums<br>- Not enough time with children<br>- Handicapped child<br>- Lack of respect for parents or teachers<br>- Having to love and look after stepchildren<br>- Transporting children to schools and other places of activity<br>- Poor academic performance<br>- Bad behaviour at school<br>- Children untidy rooms<br>- Children playing loud music that drives parents mad<br>- Late night parties<br>- Children in trouble with or with drug problems<br>- Teenage daughter who might be pregnant | |

Copyright 2022 VirtuallyThrive

## Chapter 7
## GET TO KNOW YOUR STRESSORS

Our stressors are part of our daily life. Using the table below, on the left handside highlight 4 most common stressors in your life. Then, using space on the right side write down 3 ways you will try to reduce the impact of this stressor on your life.

| Examples of Domestic Stressors | New Way of Approaching This |
|---|---|
| **Other domestic and social stressors**<br>• To marry or not<br>• Single-parent family<br>• Divorce<br>• Ageing parents<br>• Amending in-laws<br>• Unplanned pregnancy<br>• To have or not to have children<br>• Relatives with unreasonable expectations<br>• Sharing gardening, house decorating and other chores<br>• Difficult neighbours<br>• Sharing a house with relatives | |

Copyright 2022 VirtuallyThrive

# Chapter 8
## SPOTTING NEGATIVE PHRASES

Think of a stressful event or a situation that occurs regularly. What is the usual thing you say to yourself when it happens? Using space below write down 3 negative phrases you often use when speaking to yourself, when others don't listen. Then in the line below write a counter argument, something positive you can think about. See examples provided. This will make you aware of the power of your inner voice.

Examples:

Negative: *"I'm such a looser..."*
Positive: *"I dont always get it right, but i always try my best..."*

Negative: *"This is just typical of me..."*
Positive: *"If I focus more i should be able to get it right next time..."*

1.......

2.......

3.......

# Chapter 9
## PRACTICING SELF-ACCEPTANCE

Self acceptance is the basis of a healthy self-esteem. Building and maintaining self acceptance is essential to developing a positive self-image.

Take an empty sheet of paper and write down:

- 3 positive statements about yourself

- 3 biggest skills or talents that you have

- 3 facts about yourself that you are the most proud of

Accepting yourself is bringing you few steps closer to developing self-confidence, which is essential to reaching your goals and improving your life.

# Chapter 9
## POSITIVE FUTURE SELF

Before you go to sleep close your eyes and imagine yourself in the future just the way you want to be.

- *How do you look ?*

- *What do you wear?*

- *Are other people with you? Who?*

- *What are you doing? (picture yourself taking part in an event you really want to take part in or a goal you really want to achieve )*

- *How do you feel?*

I hope that you have managed to do it. Don't worry if you found it hard as many people struggle with visualising themselves in the future. I encourage you to regularly practise imagining yourself in the future: achieving your goals and taking part in positive, happy events. Imagine other people being kind to you and serve you in achieving your goals. Practising positive visualisations will support you in building your positive self image, higher self- esteem and "priming" your brain to create positive experiences.

## Chapter 10
## CELEBRATE SMALL SUCCESSES

Using a table below list your goals and desired outcomes. Following that create list of rewards. These can be big life goals or small daily goals. For each completed goal come up with one reward for yourself.

| MY GOALS | DESIRED OUTCOMES | LIST OF REWARDS |
|---|---|---|
|  |  |  |

Copyright 2022 VirtuallyThrive

# Chapter 10
## FOCUS ON YOUR FUTURE

It would be great if you could have a monthly check in with yourself to check how you are doing with reaching your goals. Try to make this a regular thing.

| WHAT'S GOING WELL THIS MONTH ? | WHAT DO I NEED TO WORK ON ? |
|---|---|
| 1. HOW WOULD YOU RATE YOUR CONFIDENCE ON A SCALE 1-10? | 1. WHAT ARE YOUR BIGGEST STRUGGLES? |
| 2. WHAT GOOD HAS HAPPENED THIS MONTH? | 2. WHAT DO YOU WANT TO WORK ON NEXT? |
| 3. WHAT ARE YOU THE MOST PROUD OF? | 3. IS THERE SOMETHING YOU SHOULD DO DIFFERENTLY? |

Copyright 2022 VirtuallyThrive

## CHEAT SHEETS

Chapter 1    Conflicting Priorities

Chapter 2    Using Your Brain - Dos and Don'ts

Chapter 3    Examples of Core Beliefs
             Beliefs, Rules and Assumptions (part 1)
             Beliefs, Rules and Assumptions (part 2)

Chapter 4    Healthy Relationships

Chapter 5    Building a Strong Support Network

Chapter 6    Confidence Boosting Words
             Confidence Killing Words

Chapter 7    Golden Nuggets of Wisdom

Chapter 8    Supportive Inner Voice

Chapter 9    Becoming Your Own Best Friend

Chapter 10   Grounding Meditation

# Chapter 1
## CONFLICTING PRIORITIES

Sometimes, in life we might get confused about which direction to go. We might get confused about our priorities or values. When this occurs, be kind to yourself and try to find your focus again.

**Below are few steps that can help in regaining this focus**

- Don't give into the pressure that society or a family might put on you.
- Observe yourself and become more self-aware.
- Pay attention to how you react in the absence of things that are important to you.
- Complete Value Determination Test by Dr. John Demartini.
- Once you know your values, find time everyday to do something that is important to you. Prioritise things that matter the most.
- Don't rely on others to tell you which direction to take in life. You know this best.
- Learn to prioritise your needs, instead of putting other people's needs first.
- Everyone has days when they are confused or tired, or days when emotions are running high. When this happens, take time out to rest, relax and regain your clarity.
- Develop a kind inner voice. Listen to this voice when you are unsure what to do.

# Chapter 2
## USING YOUR BRAIN - DOs and DON'Ts

### DOs

1. Expect the best from people and events
2. Imagine achieving best results
3. Visualise positive case scenarios
4. Practise positive affirmations
5. Talk at length about things you really want
6. Picture yourself doing great things
7. Always have positive expectations
8. Make lists of things you want
9. Every day write down 3 things you are grateful for
10. Every time something great happens, tell as many people as possible
11. Think of the presence of things you want to happen in the future
12. Pay attention to things and people that make you happy
13. Write down a future life script where you achieve everything you desire
14. Imagine people's behaviour to improve and it will.

### DON'Ts

1. Don't talk about what makes you angry or sad
2. Don't spend time discussing things you don't want to happen
3. Don't expect other people to behave badly
4. Don't focus on the negative outcomes of future events
5. Don't predict worse case scenarios
6. Don't plan and prepare for worst case scenarios
7. Don't spend time with people who don't believe in you
8. Don't ever prioritise things based on someone's expectations
9. Don't listen to others complaining about the things they are not happy about
10. Don't try to give advise or solution to these people as it will not help
11. Don't waste your life staying in a job that makes you unhappy
12. When feeling low - don't feel sorry for yourself, instead engage in new interesting activity

Copyright 2022 VirtuallyThrive

# Chapter 3
## EXAMPLES OF CORE BELIEFS

**Hopeless core beliefs are things like**
- I'm weak
- I'm out of control
- I'm a failure
- I'm not good enough
- I'm a loser

**Unlovable core beliefs are things like**
- I'm unlovable
- I'm not likable
- I'm unattractive
- I'm different from other people
- I'm bound to be alone

**Worthless core beliefs are things like**
- I'm worthless
- I'm a waste of time
- I'm not good at anything

**Negative core beliefs about the world are things like**
- the world is dangerous
- the world is unfair
- life is too hard
- things are stacked against me
- the future is hopeless

**Negative core beliefs about other people are things like**
- the people I love will always end up leaving me
- you can't count on other people
- people will always let you down
- people only care about themselves
- it's not safe to trust other people
- if you want something done you need to do it yourself

# Chapter 3
# BELIEFS, RULES AND ASSUMPTIONS

Some of the common beliefs, rules and assumptions among women are:

Examples of limiting beliefs

- *The people I love take everything I do for granted*
- *You can't ever count on other people*
- *People only care about themselves*
- *Having a business is very hard*
- *It's better not to tell the truth as people will use it against me.*
- *My friends don't care about me*

Examples of limiting rules

- *I must do everything right*
- *I should try to make everyone happy*
- *My house must always be clean*
- *I should always be prepared for the worst*
- *I must always be present at dinner time*
- *I must take care of everyone*

# Chapter 3
## BELIEFS, RULES AND ASSUMPTIONS

Examples of negative assumptions

- *If I'm always nice to everyone then people will like me*
- *If my marriage ends then I'll be alone forever*
- *If I don't do something myself it will never be done*
- *If they cared about me then they would ask how I was doing*

Negative core beliefs about the world are things such as

- *The world is dangerous*
- *The world is unfair*
- *Life is too hard*
- *Things are stacked against me*
- *The future is hopeless*

Negative core beliefs about other people are things like

- *The people I love will always end up leaving me*
- *You can't count on other people*
- *People will always let you down*
- *People only care about themselves*
- *It's not safe to trust other people*
- *Others are out to get me.*

# Chapter 4
## HEALTHY RELATIONSHIPS

We have put together few simple facts about relationships. Read them and decide which ones resonate with you most. Try to select couple you will stick to in your daily life.

1. Taking good care of yourself will make you take better care of your business and your family.
2. Make decisions based on your own feelings and not by what others might say. Your self-image and feeling of personal worth come from within.
3. When we feel good about ourselves, the behaviour of other people doesn't bother us so much. Try and keep your self-image high through positive self-talk.
4. Everyday you can be your best friend or your worst enemy. Which one do you choose?
5. Practise gratitude. Instead of focusing on what you don't have, be thankful for what you do have. Gratitude opens our hearts to more love and happiness.
6. Learn to count your blessings, not your misfortunes. Majority of our misery comes from us thinking about what you should have, instead of appreciating what you do have.
7. Find ways to give and receive love. Express your appreciation with flowers, "thank-you" letters or small unexpected gifts. This will encourage others to return this kindness to you.
8. Remind yourself that giving and receiving love is not a sign of weakness but a source of spiritual growth that we have all be seeking unconsciously since childhood.
9. A good way to reach people's hearts is to express that you appreciate their talents or recognise their importance. If you succeed in making people feel important, they will go out of their way to help you.
10. Our reactions depend on our attitudes and beliefs. Don't fall into the trap of trying to be perfect. Perfectionism is self-destructive thing. It also leads to unnecessary stress and unhappiness.

Copyright 2022 VirtuallyThrive

# Chapter 4
## HEALTHY RELATIONSHIPS

11. You need to build some fun and play into your daily schedule. This will greatly improve your relationships.

12. Little courteous phrases like, "I'm so sorry to trouble you", "Would you be so kind..." "Would you mind...", "Thank you" show your respect to others. They will also help in getting people to cooperate.

13. Learn to accept things you can't change. There is no point in getting upset over and over again about other people's behaviour which are beyond your control.

14. During a busy day stop for a minute and ask yourself: "How can I take better care of myself and listen to my inner wisdom?". This technique will help you cultivate self-trust and find an answer within yourself.

15. Develop a sense of humour and learn to laugh at imperfections. Laughing makes us feel healthy, happy and humane. It also helps us attract new friends and eases tention in our relationships.

16. When we grow apart in marriage or other relationships there is a tendency to believe that we could be happy if only the other one was more considerate. The secret lies in loving yourself. When you are happy within yourself, you give others love, respect and attention they deserve and you get the same things back.

# Chapter 5
## BUILDING A SUPPORT NETWORK

Having a strong support network is very important, especially when trying to improve or introduce change to your life.

Below are few simple steps on how to start building your support network.

- **Step One** - building positive self- image and self-esteem

- **Step Two** - setting goals, deciding what I want to achieve or change and why?

- **Step Three** - writing down how my current circle of friends support me in my goals, in the goals I want to achieve, in the plans I want to make reality? How do current people present in my life support me in that?

- **Step Four** - connecting with people who have similar goals, strive for similar things, or perhaps have already succeeded in this. If you don't know anyone like that then look at your current circle and write down who is most likely to support you and who is less likely to support you?

During this process you might realise that you spend lots of time with people who don't support you or show no interest in your plans.

# Chapter 6
## CONFIDENCE BOOSTING WORDS

Here are some words and phrases that you can include in your daily conversations with your child to boost their confidence. Read them through and try adding some of your own ones to this list.

- Definitely
- Trust
- Strength
- Courage
- Strong
- Absolutely
- Surely
- Of course
- Undeniably
- Yes
- Undoubtedly
- I know you will do it
- I'm so proud of you
- Are you proud of yourself?
- Has anyone told you that you are amazing
- I am sure you will do it
- I can guarantee it will be perfect
- I believe in you
- Believe in yourself
- This sounds like a great idea
- Wow that's a great choice
- I love it
- Thank you so much

# Chapter 6
## CONFIDENCE KILLING WORDS

You have to be aware of the language you use with a child on day-to-day basis as we will share with you some words that kill confidence over time. The words need to be avoided:

### 1. TRY/ATTEMPT

When you say you were trying to do something it has a connotation of lack of self-esteem. So when you're talking to children

**Avoid Saying** *"you have to try doing this task". Instead encourage them with words like "give it a go" or "I know you can do it and I'm here to support you"*

### 2. BUT

Eliminate the use of this word from your conversations; it negates everything you said beforehand.

**Don't say:**
*"You've done that well but next time you can add a picture to illustrate your idea."*

**Say:**
*"You have done really well and next time you could think about adding a picture to illustrate your idea too"*

### 3. HOPE

We use and hear this word all the time even when we are associated with highly optimistic people. While that might be true in most cases, for some the meaning can be a little different and less confident

**Don't say**
*I hope you will do well in the test*

**Say**
*I believe in you and I know you will do well in the test*

# Chapter 6
## CONFIDENCE KILLING WORDS

### 4. WOULD
Would, when used regarding the future, means there is some amount of confidence lacking.

**Don't say**
*You would do well in a musical lesson*

**Say**
*You will do well in music lessons*

### 5. COULD
The word could have the connotation that something is stopping or limiting a person.

**Don't say**
*You could ride that bike*

**Say**
*You can ride that bike today*

### 6. SHOULD
When you use this word with a child you put pressure on them. They feel like they is expectation attached to what you just said

**Don't say**
*You should come running with me*

**Say**
*You can come running with me*

# Chapter 6
## CONFIDENCE KILLING WORDS

### 7. WISH
Wish can show a lack of mindset

**Don't say**
*Do you wish to win the competition?*

**Say**
*Do you want to win the competition?*

### 8. NEVER
Avoid using this word no matter what you are discussing

**Don't say**
*You will never know because you are not trying*

**Say**
*Anything is possible if you try*

### 9. BUSY
We wear this word like a badge. It defines where you place your priorities. Overusing the word "busy" can make your child feel like they are constantly at the end of your to-do list.

**Don't say**
*I'm too busy to play with you right now. Go and watch the TV.*

**Say**
*I'm finishing this task which will take me five minutes and then I will take you to the park and we can play football together*

# Chapter 7
## NUGGETS OF WISDOM

We have put together few "nuggets of wisdom" about stress. Read them and decide which ones resonate with you most. Try to select few you will stick to in your daily life.

1. Learn to differentiate between minor irritations and major provocations and when not to respond to situations in a reactive way.
2. Learn to become aware of your tension levels and use stress management skills to control tension until you have developed strong coping skills.
3. Use coping skills to prepare for stressful situations, as well as to meet those that come to you unexpectedly.
4. Just as you cannot learn to drive a car by reading a book you cannot learn stress management until you regularly use stress management skills in real-life situations and are prepared to give yourself enough time and opportunity to practise those skills.
5. Physical relaxation is an effective stress management skill. Relax your tense muscles and save energy for more important things.
6. When you are feeling overwhelmed by multiple demands and little time, being snappy, using bad language or raising your voice, can only make things worse. Please remember that.
7. Many stressful situations are regular events in life. Like waiting in a queue or commuting to work. Predicting them and either avoiding them or taking effective preventative action can significantly reduce your stress levels. Therefore making your life more enjoyable.
8. Each one of us has our own stress signals telling us we are out of control. They should be used as a reminder to take one deep breath and let go of physical tension.
9. Learning new habits takes time. At times we will revert back to our old ways, but we should not lose heart. Learning and relearning is often necessary to improve quality of your life.

Copyright 2022 VirtuallyThrive

## Chapter 8
## SUPPORTIVE INNER VOICE

Much of our stress is due to silent conversations we have with ourselves. Psychologists call this **SELF-TALK**. We are able to talk ourselves into the ground by programming ourselves negatively.

Self-esteem and vulnerability are inversely related:
When self-esteem is high, vulnerability is low and vice versa.

Some people call this our critical inner voice. Everyone has this critical inner voice but people with low self-esteem have a particularly vicious one. Critical inner voice and poor self image often leads to a feeling of helplessness, which turns into helpless behavior and even depression.

Work on building your healthy self-esteem and you will find it much easier to **develop a kind and more supportive inner voice.**

This inner voice is essential to motivate you, when you need to stay focused on your goals and will act as a voice of a friend when you need it the most. Avoid negative self-talk as much as possible as it can prevent you from introducing changes to your life, taking needed action and therefore it can prevent you from improving your life and getting better life satisfaction

# Chapter 9
## BECOMING YOUR BEST FRIEND

In a world where we constantly strive to prove ourselves and gain approval from others, it's very important to be your best friend. Relying on others for the feeling of self-worth and acceptance can only be effective in the short term. All of us have days when we lack confidence or feel anxious. Being kind and gentle to yourself during days like this is even more important. This is when you should try to re- focus on self-care.

Below are few tips how to do this. If you are not sure where to start follow these simple steps:

- Go to sleep earlier than usual
- Find 15 minutes for yourself before your children wake up
- Reconnect with nature: go for a walk or spend time outside
- Find time to meditate and reconnect with yourself
- When you are alone light a candle and find time to be still and enjoy your own company.
- Listen to relaxing music or engage in creative activity
- Write down 3 things you are grateful for each day

# Chapter 10
## GROUNDING MEDITATION

Before your child begins the online class homework you can ask them to take part in the meditation to become more grounded. Grounding meditation is an excellent method to clear the mind of any clutter before starting work on anything. This meditation can be used for children and adults. This meditation is going to help you both. You as a parent or teacher will also feel refreshed and focused. Grounding meditation will also help get rid of any tension or stress that you don't want to carry into the class.. A simple script for grounding practice.

- Begin by taking a seated posture with your legs crossed.
- The posture should let your body be in contact with the ground. If you are sitting in a chair ensure that your feet are connecting with the ground.
- This practice is ideal to do in the garden before the class.
- Close your eyes and focus on the breath. For a few moments simply notice the inhales and exhales.
- Then make the inhales and exhales longer and deeper.
- Feel your connection with the core of the earth.
- Imagine your feet growing out roots and reaching to the centre of the earth.
- Picture these roots wrapping around the centre of the earth.
- Feel a sense of complete grounded-ness as you connect more and more with energy and wisdom of the earth.
- Bring your awareness back to the breath.
- Take three deep cycles of inhales and exhales.
- Come back to the awareness and the space around you.
- Open your eyes and sit still for a moment as you come out of the meditation.
- Notice how you feel.

## SUGGESTION BOARDS

Chapter 1   Knowing Your Values

Chapter 2   Being conscious of your words

Chapter 3   Using Meta Model

Chapter 4   Communication in Relationships

Chapter 5   Connecting with others based on common goals

Chapter 6   Empowering Your Kids to Thrive

Chapter 7   Manage Your Stress

Chapter 8   Developing Kind Inner Voice

Chapter 9   Positive Visualisations

Chapter 10 Making Progres

SUGGESTION BOARD
# CHAPTER 1

## Knowing Your Values

Not many of us know our values, yet this is an essential step if you are looking for more happiness or better life satisfaction. It's worth investing time to understand what your Values System is based on.

We recommend that you take part in Value Determination Process by Dr. John Demartini. You can complete the process here https://drdemartini.com/values/

Once you know what your values are you can live a more purposeful life, and will be able to focus on what is really important to you, instead of prioritising the needs of others as a default.

This is your life so take charge of what you do everyday and fill your day with tasks and activities that bring you joy and fulfilment.

Copyright 2022 VirtuallyThrive

SUGGESTION BOARD
# CHAPTER 2

## Being conscious of your words

Words can be very powerful if we know how to use them to our advantage.

We all have days when we feel quite negative. If you find yourself often saying statements as: "I never have any time for myself", or "My days are filled with things I don't want to do" - remind yourself that what you are saying is only confirming a negative belief that is stored in your mind, therefore it's not going to serve you at all. Instead try saying things like:

"In the past, I couldn't find time for myself but I've learned to plan better so now I can always find an hour per week to do what I really love."

You can say similar statements in the past tense to deal with other limiting beliefs. This will help you to boost your self-confidence and "prime" your brain for more positive experiences.

Copyright 2022 VirtuallyThrive

SUGGESTION BOARD
## CHAPTER 3

# Using Meta Model

A limiting belief is a mindset or thought pattern that a person believes to be their reality. Beliefs rule our thinking and our behaviours. If you lack confidence based on your limiting beliefs, you can understand yourself better by observing your own behaviour. Another great way to transform negative self-talk is to challenge your feelings by asking questions, such as :

- What causes me to feel that way?
- When do I feel like that?
- When don't I feel like that?
- What would I like to feel instead?

This is self-observation technique will help you deal with negative feelings you experience regularly.

Copyright 2022 VirtuallyThrive

SUGGESTION BOARD
# CHAPTER 4

# Communication in Relationships

Communicating is not always easy. We have put together a few suggestions to help you on your way.

1. Being irritable and impatient towards others leads them to mirror your response and creates a negative spiral of escalating tension. Raising your voice or shouting at your partner or your child increases the stress you are already experiencing. So try to avoid it and stay calm.

2. Don't bottle up emotions or lose control. Instead, try practising effective communication. Try different things and learn what works and what doesn't.

3. Before you speak up or respond to someone ask yourself: "Do I really have something to say?" or "Will speaking up make things better?" All of us experience conflict in our relationships but it's how you interpret and respond to the other person that makes the whole difference.

Copyright 2022 VirtuallyThrive

SUGGESTION BOARD
# CHAPTER 5

## Connecting with others based on common goals

We all have friends and family but only some of us are using our network to really help our growth. Connecting with people who have similar goals to you is a good way to get inspiration and motivation. Look for people who show interest in what you are trying to achieve. If you don't know anyone like that then look at your current circle of friends and write down who is most likely to support you and who is likely to make you feel doubtful about yourself or makes you more confused or anxious.

This simple exercise might help you realise that you spend too much time with people who don't support you and show no interest in your plans or goals. In which case you might be better off to invest in new friendships and expand your network.

Copyright 2022 VirtuallyThrive

SUGGESTION BOARD
# CHAPTER 6

## Empowering Your Kids to Thrive

It's very important for mums to encourage their children, to build positive self - image and healthy self - esteem. There are many things you can do to archive that.

Below are few ideas where to start:

- Actively listen to them, - Provide a safe and open home environment, where everyone is accepted for who they are, - Avoid labels such as "depressed" or "anxious" as they might be too foreign to a child. Instead use "sad" and "scared", - Let your child express their emotions at all times and talk about them with you, - Build a strong relationship with your child where you both open up to your weaknesses and you acknowledge them, - Always try to model healthy behaviour, - Try to stay calm during arguments and heated family discussions, - Give your kids hugs and show them love every day, - Teach communication and coping skills, - Encourage your partner to support "no mental health stigma" home environment, - Teach your kids to build a positive self-image

Copyright 2022 VirtuallyThrive

SUGGESTION BOARD
# CHAPTER 7

## Manage Your Stress

Stress is present in our lives daily and nobody is immune to it. Learning to manage stressful situations that occur regularly can make your life so much easier and more enjoyable. It will also help take pressure off your relationships. Below are a few simple suggestions that should help manage stress better.

1. Schedule "ME" time in your calendar. Make sure you schedule time away from your partner, your children and house chores. Find 20 minutes each day to do something enjoyable, something "just for you". This will help you deal with stressful situations when they occur. You will also feel more "in control" of your life.

2. Develop a good evening routine. Learn to meditate and quiet your mind before you go to sleep. Don't get involved in serious conversations or watching a scary film right before you go to bed. Gentle stretches, a warm bath, a relaxing tea or listening to some nice soothing music will help you get into a restful night's sleep.

3. Allow enough time to sleep and rest everyday. We all underestimate the importance of sleep and physical rest. Yet this is so essential to staying balanced and focused.

Copyright 2022 VirtuallyThrive

SUGGESTION BOARD
# CHAPTER 8

## Developing Kind Inner Voice

You might not think about yourself as your biggest supporter but remember that others will come and go and you have yourself for the rest of your life. You are always there for yourself and should trust yourself especially in difficult life situations. This is why it's important that you become your own best friend and build a supportive inner voice. In order to build a positive inner voice you need to practise it regularly. Try below excercize to practise it.

Take an empty sheet of paper and write a kind letter addressed to yourself. Write it as if you were writing to your best friend. Use soft and encouraging tone and kind words. Thank yourself for doing so very well every day and having your own back. Suggest what else you can do to support yourself in the future in raising your self-esteem and developing this supportive inner voice.

Copyright 2022 VirtuallyThrive

SUGGESTION BOARD
# CHAPTER 9

## Positive Visualisations

Relying on others to feel good about yourself is not an effective long term solution. The key is to Accept Yourself for Who You Are and Become Your Best Friend. However, it's easier said than done. If you don't know how to boost your self-confidence or improve your self-image, try using positive visualisations.

Find a quiet moment in your day or in the evening. Make sure you are not disturbed. Close your eyes and imagine yourself in the future doing something you love. It could be having a dream job, practising a hobby that you never have time for, or simply being on holiday in a beautiful place. How does it feel? Really embrace the feelings that you experience in this moment. Why not making this a habit and practise positive visualisations daily? This will help you boost your self confidence and will bring you closer to reaching your future goals. Mind is like a muscle - the more you practise it the more powerful it gets.

Copyright 2022 VirtuallyThrive

SUGGESTION BOARD
# CHAPTER 10

## Making Progress

1. If you have many tasks to complete, divide the work into segments before deciding what you need to finish on a specific day. You might feel overwhelmed if you scheduled too much in a short space of time. This will result in burnout and stress.

2. Try to stay away from multitasking. Instead focus on one task at a time. It's very difficult to juggle between house chores, child's homework, and checking your emails at once.

3. Remember to take breaks and give yourself space to breathe. If you just came home from work, take few minutes to yourself, before you dive into something new. This will help to clear your mind and help prevent you from getting overwhelmed.

4. Use affirmations daily to help you stay motivated when things get hard. Positive affirmations have been proved to be very effective when used regularly.